Giving Your Child an Edge

A Parenting Handbook

by JoAnn Flammer

Lone Loon Press

Adirondack   New York   USA

Giving Your Child an Edge
A Parenting Handbook

Visit the author at:
joannflammer.com

ISBN: 978-0-615-25550-7

Lone Loon Press
Adirondack, NewYork

Printed in the United States of America

*This book is dedicated
to all the parents
who are smart enough
to learn from their children.*

Acknowledgements

Many thanks to Nancy O'Brien, former editor of the *Adirondack Journal* for listening to my idea for a column and then actually printing *Giving Your Child an Edge* for consumption by the parents, grandparents, and other caregivers in our community, and to Thom Randall, present editor of the *Adirondack Journal*, for continuing to find room for my columns within the journal's jam-packed pages.

The professors at Dowling College were a major influence in shaping my philosophy for teaching as were the following favorite authors: Hornsby, Sukarna, and Parry, *Read on: A Conference Approach to Reading*; William Glasser, *Control Theory in the Classroom*; E.D. Hirsch, Jr., *Cultural Literacy*; Peter Kline, *Everyday Genius*; and Frank Smith, *Understanding Reading*.

I cannot forget the faculty, staff, and parents at Brook Avenue School in Bay Shore, Long Island, New York, and especially my students who challenged me daily to be the teacher I am today.

Finally, I owe the most to my three daughters, Kathleen, Sandra, and Deborah, who taught me the wonders of parenting and being a mom, and to Lee, my husband, best friend, and parenting partner for his never ending encouragement and love.

Dear Parents,

You are your children's primary teachers. It's up to you to see that they receive the best education ... one that guarantees them a successful, productive place in the community and the world.

Whenever I met with the parents of my elementary aged students, they would inevitably ask what they could do at home to help their children. There was never enough time at these meetings to go into specifics, so I always said: read, read, read. Fortunately, Brook Avenue School and the PFA recognized parents' needs and held workshops for them. I led a number of parenting workshops on reading, writing, and spelling to encourage parents to participate in their children's learning at home. Much of the information I shared with parents at those workshops is printed in this handbook.

As a retired teacher, I continue to work with elementary aged children, and I'm hearing the same question from parents: What can we do to help our children at home? So, I began to write a column for the local paper. I was so encouraged by the response and positive feedback from parents, grandparents, and teachers alike that I decided to compile the columns into a book, this book, Giving Your Child an Edge, A Parenting Handbook.

I encourage you to read the tips, strategies, and suggestions within these pages, but don't feel overwhelmed. You cannot do everything today, or even tomorrow. Try working a few ideas into your daily lives and see the difference it makes. When a strategy becomes automatic, try another and another until you and your children have made learning a priority, a family adventure, and fun.

Your children's teachers normally know them only ten months out of their lives; you have them forever. You can be the person in their life who makes a difference, who gives them an edge, who helps them discover that learning is fun and natural and within reach because you are there for them.

Sincerely,
JoAnn Flammer

Table of Contents

Acknowledgements
Dear Parents

One Reading   page 1

1. Read it again, please! 2
   How to promote and reinforce reading skills for toddlers
   and beginning readers

2. "I read you loud and clear!"   4
   Reading is comprehension.

3. Raising a lifelong reader   7
   Make your children 'thirsty' for reading.

4. 'When the bough breaks…'   9
   Phonics is not always the best way to decode a word.

Two Vocabulary   page 13

5. Vocabulary is key to a child's development.   14
   Talking to your children builds an extensive receptive
   vocabulary.

6. Building a Word Bank   16
   Reading taps into other people's vocabularies.

7. Communicating through speaking and writing   18
   How to build an expressive vocabulary.

Three Spelling   page 23

8.   prvt cep owt   24
Conventional spelling develops the same way speech develops.

Four Prior Knowledge   page 29

9.   What every child needs to know 30
Authors assume readers have a store of traditional, historical, and cultural facts.

10. Teaching children to relate to what they know   32
Model previewing, predicting, and self-questioning as your read to your children.

Five Summer Fun   page 37

11. Don't let your children fall behind this summer.   38
Children who read throughout the summer gain reading skills.

12. Boost your children's confidence in math.   40
Games and activities that strengthen math skills

Six Behavior   page 45

13. What kind of parent are you?   46
Maintain a balance between strict and lenient while fostering independence

14. Challenging 'bored' children   48
Kindle imaginations and encourage active thinking

About the Author

One
Reading

Read it again, please!

"Read it again, pleeeeeze," whines your child for the umpteenth time. You moan and suggest another book—well don't. Just read it again…and again…and again! Repetition is fundamental to learning to read.

First of all, this book apparently has your child's interest, so use it to promote and reinforce reading skills: which word do you think is 'ball'? as you stress the 'b' sound; match words to the pictures on the page or cover; point out word patterns such as rhyming (words with similar endings) or alliteration (words that begin the same); pause as you read and see if your child can 'read' the next word, which he undoubtedly will do because he's pretty much memorized the entire book by now.

Second, reading books over and over builds sight vocabulary and imprints words permanently into those receptive vocabulary files[1], ready and waiting to be called upon for future reading.

But there are many ways to bring repetition into your children's reading besides rereading a book:

- To reinforce and build on known vocabulary, keep with a theme when choosing books. Select all animal books, books about winter, or same character books like Winnie the Pooh.
- Stock up on poetry books and stories that use rhyming with word families (cat, bat, hat) so your children can predict words that are coming and participate in the reading.
- Predicting as you read (What do you think will happen next?) helps children realize that the words the author has chosen are everyday words, their words, words already in their heads. Plus they feel proud when their prediction is confirmed.
- Try Echo Reading with your children. Read a sentence and ask them to read it back to you. This activity not only gives them confidence in reading, but builds sight vocabulary and encourages them to pay attention to the words you're reading.

However, while promoting and reinforcing reading skills are important, the main thing when reading with your children is to HAVE FUN! Don't let reading become boring or humdrum or a chore. Knock on the table if the character knocks on a door; change your voice to match characters' feelings; laugh aloud when the character laughs. Have fun and let reading time become an enjoyable activity for all.

[1]Read about receptive vocabulary in section TWO.

~ 2 ~

"I read you, loud and clear!"

Whether you're reading a person, reading a map, reading between the lines, reading sign language, reading a recipe, or reading the newspaper, your purpose is the same—to understand, to comprehend—to get it!

Can you read this aloud?

Did Alfred bran quirky when he plowed the phat?

Sorry…you're not reading, you're word calling. Sure, you can say all the words and even be expressive with the question mark, but you cannot make sense out of them. Unfortunately, that's what some children do. They read an entire page without stumbling over a single word. It sounds perfect, but they have no idea what they read.

So how do you know if your child is reading or word calling? Easy. Ask questions that promote understanding and listen for signs that your child comprehends.

Trying to keep dry, Jamie huddled under the Spiderman
umbrella as he waited for the bus
to take him to his first day of kindergarten.

Is Jamie a boy or a girl? What is the weather? Where is Jamie going? The words boy, rainy, and school are not written but inferred, requiring the reader to extract meaning from the text. How old do you think Jamie is? What do you think Jamie will do in school? Open-ended questions (any reasonable answer) encourage children to predict, confirm prediction and give purpose to reading on. If you ask a yes/no question, follow it with 'Why do you think that?' Eventually self-questioning will become automatic, a part of the reading process, and your child's reading comprehension will increase.

For children, reading aloud is like cold-reading to an actor…no practice so they're not sure where the emphasis goes or what mood the author is trying to create. Nevertheless, reading aloud an important tool in discovering the reading strategies being used. Do they self-correct, re-read to make sense, and use punctuation?

Good readers don't read one word at a time. Their eyes actually scan ahead four or five words. So, children who say 'can't' instead of 'cannot' or Dad instead 'father' have read ahead, anticipated what's next, and used appropriate substitutions. In their effort to comprehend the text, children who read ahead sometimes omit words they've judged insignificant to the meaning. There's no need to interrupt the reader's flow for changed or missing words unless they interfer with the meaning.

If your children pause, don't rush in with the word. Some words like bow, tear, and wind cause the reader to hesitate and determine which meaning makes sense before choosing which pronunciation to use. Give them 'wait time' to figure it out on their own.

In conclusion, while expression and fluency are important

indicators of good readers, they are not the final assessment. Remember, you are not listening for the perfect word caller, but you are listening for signs that your child is understanding, comprehending—getting it!

Raising a lifelong reader

You can lead a child to the library, but you can't make him read. Ahhhh, but you can make him 'thirsty' for reading.

First, create a climate for reading so your children associate reading with pleasure. Tempt children to curl up with a good book in a quiet, comfy room filled with soft beanbag chairs, fluffy body pillows, cozy comforters for cuddling or stretching out on the floor.

Good lighting keeps readers' eyes from becoming tired and droopy. Supply table lamps, floor lamps, personal book lamps, even flashlights for that ghost book or mystery.

Set the tone for reading with a variety of books, newspapers and magazines spread out on tables and shelves around the room. Entice children with their own magazine subscriptions, and watch their enthusiasm for reading grow as magazines arrive in the mail.

Give your children a sense of power over their reading with their own library cards. Then provide opportunities to 'choose' their reading material with frequent trips to the library. Encourage them to vary the books they borrow: picture books, mysteries, fables, biographies, and how-to books. Poetry, jokes, rhymes, and riddles will captivate even the reluctant reader. Help them select books they are capable of reading by applying the 'five-finger rule' where if a child can't read five words on a page, the book is too hard for independent reading.

Next, develop a family reading tradition by setting aside a special reading time for everyone. This could be shared reading where you and your children take turns reading aloud, or silent reading where you respect each other's right to quiet. Even your youngest child can sit and 'read' silently, enjoying pictures and text patterns in a book. It is very important that your children see you reading silently and getting pleasure from a book or magazine.

Finally, show your children that you care about their reading. Discuss what they've read: was it funny, sad, informative? Ask them the how and why of their reading choices. If you are not happy with some of their selections, don't put them down; encourage them to try different genres. Let them know they can start a book or article and not finish it if it doesn't interest them.

Making reading a priority in your home establishes the importance of reading and will turn your children into lifelong readers.

And lifelong readers are lifelong learners.

~ **4** ~

'When the bough breaks...'

"I'm stuck on a word," calls your eight-year-old from across the room. "Sound it out," you call back as you transfer laundry from washer to dryer. "What does 'gh' say?" You think: /g/ in ghost or /f/ in tough or nothing in light.

Clearly, in this instance, phonics—a sounding-out challenge in itself—won't work. The English language has scores of words that do not follow the rules. As your children's reading levels advance, they need to apply more sophisticated strategies for decoding unfamiliar words.

Most words children read are actually known words that they've heard but not read before. One of the most effective strategies is to read on and make use of the rest of the text. Say blank for the unfamiliar word and read to the end of the sentence. Then go back, read the sentence again, and most of the time your children will recognize the word. Sometimes, they may need to read further back or ahead more, but usually the surrounding words will provide enough clues to crack the code.

Another practical approach is looking at the pictures or

graphics on the page. The labels in diagrams point to relevant information and help the reader figure out challenging words. Illustrations usually correspond to the written text and jog the reader's memory.

The letter arrangement of a word is telling, too. Suggest examining the word for familiar chunks or word families such as –ight in might, tight, right; look for smaller words within the word; cover up suffixes like -ed and -ing at the end of words and prefixes, un- or re- at the beginning.

Guide your children to consider what the story or passage is about. For instance, for 'bough' in the Rock-a-bye Baby nursery rhyme, ask where the baby is and try substituting another word that makes sense, such as 'When the branch breaks.' Then reread to see if this nudges their memory. Sometimes, background knowledge or familiarity with the content helps. Your child may have heard the nursery rhyme from you or another relative and remember hearing 'bough.'

But don't let your children spend too much time figuring out unfamiliar or unknown words or they will lose the meaning of the entire passage. Sometimes, the best strategy is for you to just walk over and tell your child the word.

Strategies in Place

Observations

Evaluation

Two
Vocabulary

~ 5 ~

Key to a child's development

An extensive vocabulary is the key to a child's success in listening and reading as well as speaking and writing. Children learn new words rapidly and effortlessly, so let's look at ways to expand their receptive vocabulary, the vocabulary acquired from listening and reading.

Start with a very simple, but very effective, activity: TALKING to your children. You're going to think, Oh, this is silly, but it's not. Talking increases and enhances a child's vocabulary file, especially if you don't 'dumb down' your language because you're talking to a child. Talk as you would to an adult. If your children need clarification, they'll ask! Even if they don't ask, you've deposited another word or expression in their brain's file folder, ready for use when needed in listening or reading.

Talk, as an activity, has many advantages:
- You don't need to schedule time to talk.
- You don't need a special place to talk.
- You don't need to gather any materials for this activity.

Just talk…while you're cooking, driving, giving baths, doing laundry, walking from the car to the store…anytime!

Say things like: Grandpa is a veteran. He fought in the Vietnam War. Now you've given your child 'veteran' and even its meaning. Share your childhood events; recite nursery rhymes; sing songs you sang as a child; talk about your career; discuss the weather. And if your conversation doesn't happen to include any new words, you are still reinforcing known or everyday words.

The more your children hear a word, the more familiar it will be, the more likely it will be launched into their expressive vocabulary, and the more apt they will be to use it to communicate in speaking and writing.

They say 'talk is cheap' but in this case talk will raise your children to a higher level of thinking and doing!

~ 6 ~

Building a Word Bank

Reading to or with your children has a major impact on their receptive vocabularies. While talking to them awards them the benefit of your vocabulary, reading taps into the vast vocabularies of countless authors, thereby generating a more comprehensive word bank for your children. The more words they see in print, the more words they will be able to read and understand, which is especially important as they move on to independent reading.

But unlike talking, reading involves more of your time and resources:

- You need books, magazines, newspapers.
- You need a specific place to sit and read.
- You need to be available.

I know…you can't get to the library, you barely get the homework completed at night, your child falls asleep in his mashed potatoes—or maybe you fall asleep in your mashed potatoes. However, reading is vital to your child's future.

The good thing is that there are no set rules to follow. You don't have to read only at bedtime and you don't have to only read books. When time is limited, share recipes or a set of directions with your child as you work; share letters and e-mails from friends or relatives; read newspaper articles or ads as you go through the local papers; read aloud while you're waiting at the doctor's office; read short stories from children's magazines, poems from a children's poetry book, and jokes from a children's joke book.

Setting aside a special reading time before or after work and on your day off will give your child something to look forward to. Try to have a number of books or magazines on hand so your child has some choices. Children love to have favorite books read over and over and the repetition is excellent for depositing and saving words in their vocabularies.

The important thing to remember is that the more your children listen to you read or read with you, the bigger their word banks grow and the better readers, speakers, and writers they will become.

Communicating through speaking and writing

Most of the words your children need for communication are in their receptive vocabulary; speaking and writing add them to their expressive vocabulary.

Children usually start by saying words they have heard often and have become comfortable or familiar with, sometimes repeating them ad nauseam as they try them out in their speech. The more a word is used, the faster it becomes rooted in their expressive vocabulary. At this point in their language development, they need to feel free to take risks with pronunciations and meanings, so be gentle in your teaching. Instead of outright correcting, simply reuse the misused word appropriately as you respond to your child's dialogue.

Your children need your support and encouragement as they expand their expressive vocabulary. It's your turn to listen while they talk. And listening means paying attention so you can broaden your child's word usage by asking questions, offering comments, and supplying related words.

Of course, you won't always have the time or desire to listen after a long, hard day or if you're in the middle of something. So invest in a recorder and ask your child to tell about the day's events or just retell a favorite story into the microphone. Then share the recording during a meal or at bedtime or on the weekend.

Writing is another way children develop their expressive vocabulary: letters to Grandma (I supply stamped, self-addressed envelopes.), thank you notes, pet care instructions, and grocery lists. Create lists of words that end the same (bat, cat,) or begin the same (yellow, yard) or a list of synonyms (chair, rocker, stool) or homophones like by/buy/bye, ate/eight. Then write silly sentences, poems, or stories with the words.

Start a journal where your child writes and you respond, but be careful not to make it a spelling and grammar lesson. Your written response will silently show the correct spelling and usage. Give your child family photos to record who, what, when and where information on the back. Games, such as Scrabble or Boggle, and crossword puzzles where your child has to build the words, provide fun family times to explore and try out both familiar and new words.

A well-developed expressive vocabulary gives children the confidence to increase their quantity and quality of language use and improve their chances for academic success. However you choose to help expand your child's communication skills, remember to make it meaningful and fun!

Strategies in Place

Observations

Evaluation

Three
Spelling

~ 8 ~

privt cep owt

You cringe when you see these words posted on your six-year-old's door, not because you are barred from entering—I mean who really wants to go in there—but because you fear for your child's future. Well, fear not! What you are viewing is normal spelling development. Just as you respond to a toddler's "up" or "drink" without a lesson on speaking in complete sentences, so should you respond by knocking and showing your child you appreciate this attempt at spelling.

Children need to take risks as they write. In the draft stage, children should write what they're thinking and feeling without interrupting their train of thought and fluency with spelling concerns. If they have to spell every word correctly, their writing will be too limited to have any substance. Corrections can be made later.

But not all writing needs to be corrected—only writing that will be 'published' such as letters to Aunt Bessy and final reports for school. If you overwhelm your child with corrections, your child will be reluctant to write.

Children learn conventional spelling the same way they develop speech—by imitation. So, reading is essential to better spelling! The more words they see in print, the better spellers they become.

And of course, practice makes perfect. Keep writing materials handy. Put together a writing center with pens, pencils, markers, crayons, and pencil sharpeners. Stock different kinds of paper: lined, unlined, fancy stationery, cards, envelopes, and construction paper. Be creative. Have a dictionary available. A thesaurus is another excellent writing tool to help your children choose a variety of words and avoid the overuse of 'nice' and 'good.'

Once your writing center is set up, provide reasons to write: thank you letters, get well cards, birthday greetings, grocery lists, complaints or grievances—usually a favorite. Then share your children's writing. If it's totally unreadable, ask if you can print some of the words underneath to help you remember what they've written. Write notes to your child, keep a journal or diary where you respond (spelling correctly of course) to their entries, ask family and friends to answer letters or notes, and create all kinds of lists such as what to pack for a vacation.

Most of all, do not to panic at the spelling attempts. As adults, we depend on dictionaries, spell check, and secretaries, so give your children an edge and make content, not spelling, the priority in their writing.

Strategies in Place

Observations

Evaluation

Four

Prior Knowledge

~ 9 ~

What every child should know

Your child is reading next week's weather forecast for a homework assignment and declares:

'It says we better build an ark. What do they mean?'

Culturally literate readers recognize the reference to Noah and the great flood as common knowledge acquired in childhood and stored as background knowledge. Newspapers, magazines, and books take it for granted that their readers have this store of facts rooted in past and present history, tradition and culture. If the assumed information is not there, the reader fails to comprehend the deep meaning beneath the surface of the text.

Because of this assumed prior knowledge of people, places, and events, writers trade wordy descriptions and explanations for analogies and inferences: as tall as a skyscraper, being a Grinch, such an ugly duckling, and 'Slow and steady wins the race.' Shared knowledge helps writers get their meaning across in a more concise, picturesque manner.

By third and fourth grade, children's reading contains elements from Bible stories, classics, fairy tales, fables, and tall tales, as well as past and present day happenings. Children who have squirreled away this information grasp the deeper meaning of the text and consider reading relevant. Those who 'don't get it' question their ability to read, become discouraged and frustrated, and often give up on reading.

So, what can you do to make sure your children have the collective knowledge needed to make them successful readers? Immerse them in past and present history, tradition and culture.

Don't panic like Chicken Little. It's not as overwhelming as it sounds. Most of the assumed information is learned naturally as you go about the everyday challenge of raising your children. Reading aloud, family vacations, and holiday celebrations all shape communal knowledge; school curriculum, and teachers and classmates exchanging ideas add to and build on what children already know; games like Trivial Pursuit and Jeopardy reinforce a broad range of facts.

If you're wondering what information is actually taken for granted, books and articles on cultural literacy are available on-line, in libraries, and from book stores.

But, again, be careful. The lists are just for reference, not memorization. The ideal is for your children to become culturally literate naturally by interacting with the world around them.

As always, be supportive as your children read, encourage them to ask questions at home and at school, and provide experiences that will help them 'read between the lines' and understand the author's true meaning.

~ 10 ~

Teaching your children
to draw on what they know

As they read, adults automatically question what they read,
relate new information to past experiences, and create images
from what they know. But beginning readers need your help to
learn how to access prior knowledge.

Start with the cover of your first read-aloud book. As you and
your children examine the cover, the process of 'applying what is
known' begins. Point out pictures, illustrations, and text; relate
what they see with things they know. For example, if there's a
ball, discuss bouncing and throwing; talk about shape and color;
compare it to one in the toy box. Does the book's cover bring any
past or recent experiences to mind?
If there's a castle or dragon, ask if the story is real or make-
believe. Previewing the book activates background knowledge.

Next comes prediction. This strategy requires readers to use
what they know to generate expectations about the subject. Then,
as they read, they consider their expectations, thus reducing the
chance for misunderstanding or not comprehending. While

reading with your children, ask what they think will happen next, what characters might do that will affect the story, or what they would do if they were in the story. Then ask why they think this. Model predicting by sharing your thoughts so your children see how predicting helps the reading process. Then 'read on' to check the accuracy of all predictions. But remember, there are no right or wrong predictions—at first, guesses may be wild and crazy, but they'll become more educated as your children practice predicting under your loving guidance.

We don't only question to predict. We question to clarify and comprehend. After sharing text and illustrations with your children, use the five w's: who, what, where, when and why. This strategy helps with 'reading between the lines' and understanding deeper meanings. Why did one character call another 'an ugly duckling'? Who bakes cookies like that? Can you picture when we built our last snowman? Questioning triggers prior knowledge, creates connections that extend concepts, and facilitates the readers' grasp of important details.

So, the key to strengthening your children's reading comprehension lies with you. As you model previewing, predicting, and self-questioning, you provide opportunities for your children to observe and practice using what they know to bring meaning and understanding to text and illustrations.

Reading to and with your children is always time well spent.

Strategies in Place

Observations

Evaluation

Five
Summer Fun

~ 11 ~

Don't let your children
fall behind this summer!

As school doors close for the summer, learning not only shuts down but begins to slip backward. Just mention 'reading' and children whine and roll their eyes: "It's summer vacaaaaation."

When children don't read during the summer, their reading comprehension falls behind. They forget rules and strategies learned the previous year. Come September, teachers spend precious hours re-teaching skills lost over the summer.

But you can give your child an edge. Your support and attitude about summer reading will influence your children's motivation to read. Here are five suggestions to encourage summer reading:

1. Be a frequent visitor to local libraries; let your children load up on books they check out with their very own library card. The books should be easy to somewhat challenging, but not frustrating. Use teacher-generated summer reading lists or ask the librarian for

recommendations. Obtain a calendar of events from local libraries; then attend the many children's programs scheduled throughout the summer to promote reading and learning.

2. Form a weekly book club for your children to share books with peers. But make them fun times! If the group reads a fairy tale, help them dress up like the characters and act out the story; prepare snacks appropriate to a story, such as 'dirt cups' made out of chocolate pudding, Oreos and gummy worms after reading about gardening; read books by the same author, like Arthur books, and provide materials for writing their own Arthur books; read a book about animals and make paper bag puppets for retelling the story.

3. Choose books that match day trips or vacations you have planned. Your children will be energized reading about what they'll be seeing and doing. Or plan a trip around a book: read a detective book, then arrange a visit to the local police headquarters.

4. Choose books that have been made into movies. After reading the book, view the movie version then discuss similarities and differences. Which was better? Why?

5. Read daily as part of your routine: local newspapers, TV Guides, magazines, cookbooks, directions, and how-to books. End the day by reading to your children; even teens enjoy listening to a story.

The idea is to keep your children reading so they gain skills over the summer while discovering the satisfaction found in reading. Come September, not only will they will be better readers, they will be joyful readers, too!

~ 12 ~

Boost your children's
confidence in math.

Summer is an excellent time to boost your children's confidence in math. Knowing basic number facts and understanding number sense are essential for advanced computation. All it takes is a little ingenuity and a lot of fun to accomplish what tedious memorization and drill do. As children play math games, they develop an understanding of numbers and their relationships, forming their own system for solving problems.

'Facts for Ten' is a simple game for the whole family. Remove picture cards from a deck of playing cards and place the remaining cards face down on the table. Players take turns turning over one card at a time and picking up cards that add up to ten. Throughout the game, children are mentally clumping numbers and fixing facts in their minds; younger children see and count the dots on the card, establishing a sense of how many in a number.

For 'Button Toss,' number the bottom half of an egg carton

from 1-12. Players take turns standing back, tossing a handful (three, four, or five) of buttons into the egg carton, and mentally adding the numbers where the buttons land to determine their score. For variety, number the egg carton counting by 2's or 10's.

Money always gets a child's attention. Put a pile of change in the middle of the table. Then see how many ways your children can withdraw twenty-five cents, fifty cents, a dollar counting by two's, fives, tens, etc. They'll learn to recognize coins and their values front and back while practicing skip counting.

Play 'store' by pricing items from your cupboard with values your children can handle. Help them practice giving change for a dollar by counting up from the cost of the item…a very useful life skill.

Change the point value in ping-pong, badmitten, and throwing hoops so children have to skip count or multiply to determine the score: each basket is worth five so four baskets equals twenty points.

But don't stop here. Think up your own fun activities for estimating, rounding numbers, weights and measures, etc. All the ideas I've listed involve mental math—no pencil and paper computation—everything's done in your head using patterns and basic math facts, so children develop proficiency and strengthen number sense.

By the end of summer, your children will gain confidence in their own math ability and learn that math is fun.

Strategies in Place

Observations

Evaluation

Six
Behavior

~ 13 ~

Which kind of parent are you?

Your child is working on a school project. You walk over and say, "What a mess. Here, let me fix it." You take over and your child wanders off to play as you complete the project and clean up.

Constantly 'doing' for your child is 'enabling' your child— easier for you as a parent, but definitely harmful for the future of your child. If you continually finish or redo chores and tasks for them, children become passive, stagnating their development, and eventually grow to be unable or unwilling to complete tasks independently.

It's not always easy to praise their 'approximations' when we know it could be done better, faster, neater. But without their own efforts, their own mistakes and their own messes, they will never be better, faster, or neater!

When your children fail, become frustrated or unhappy, try to work with them, not for them. Make them accountable, facing consequences when necessary.

In short, don't cover up mistakes; don't clean up messes; don't finish homework; don't write or make excuses for them. Guide your children with loving patience. Be supportive and trusting as your children take on more and more responsibility, and give them space as they strive for independence.

So, just which kind of parent are you?

Too strict? Parents who always say 'because I said so' are not giving children the chance to make decisions and become accountable. There are times when 'because I said so' is the answer —but save it for major moments. Children with over-strict parents haven't learned to compromise or make decisions independently and are often bullies or followers who will do anything to fit in with a group.

Too permissive? Children who don't have rules to follow or expectations to meet flounder and often feel at loose ends. These children have not learned to work cooperatively and have problems conforming to school and community regulations, often resisting authority.

Just right? These parents set fair rules and attainable expectations, assign chores, follow through on consequences, and are willing to be unpopular in a loving, supportive way. They teach their children to handle frustration and face disappointment without losing self-confidence. Their children learn to compromise, consider others, and make wise choices.

This is the kind of parent we all want to be—loving, caring parents who find a balance between strict and permissive—raising kind, responsible children who are a blessing and an inspiration to any family, school, and community.

~ 14 ~

Preventing the 'I'm bored!' phase in children

Babies don't get bored. They play with their toes; they look and listen. Toddlers don't get bored. They occupy themselves with empty boxes; they explore and discover. So how do children stray from the innate ability to entertain themselves to the 'I'm bored!' phase?

Let's begin with television. It's not called 'the boob tube' for nothing. Viewers do not have to use their imagination—everything's created for them. There's no interaction and little mental stimulation. Too much television leads to inactive minds, dulled imaginations, and boredom.

Books, on the other hand, require readers to shape characters and settings using, not only text, but their own experiences and recollections. For instance, children who live in the country will imagine a different scenario or background to a story than children raised among tall buildings and noisy streets. Books expand horizons, stretch imaginations, and promote active thinkers.

Next comes role-playing. Pretending is how children practice for adulthood. They become parents, teachers, doctors, movie stars. And they don't need expensive toys for this. Their props are all over the house; they just need their imaginations. They don't even need other children. They have pets, stuffed animals, and YOU! Just sit back. Be the child, or the patient, or the student— you'd be amazed at the settings your children are capable of putting together as they run around the house gathering props. Role-playing promotes creativity and initiative.

Play the age-old games like Simon Says, I Spy, and Follow the Leader. Sing Old McDonald, The Farmer in the Dell, and Bingo. Make up mental math problems: I have three coins that add up to twenty-five cents. Play a spelling game where each person adds a letter until you complete a word: you say b, child says a, and keep going. Build a sentence one word at a time. Have a contest to see how many things can be made with a toilet paper tube. You'll find that even teens enjoy a challenge. These games, songs, and activities exercise the mind. They promote concentration, recall, deductive reasoning, problem solving, and risk-taking.

If you kindle imaginations and encourage active thinking when your children are young, they will develop the ability to continue interacting with their environment and be resourceful with their time. Boredom is monotony of the mind due to a lack of motivation and interest.

Self-motivated, inquisitive, independent thinkers who have learned to 'do' instead of having others do for them will never be bored.

Strategies in Place

Observations

Evaluation

Books We've Read Together
*Put a * next to favorites!*

About the Author

JoAnn Flammer is a freelance writer and a retired elementary teacher. Her New York teaching certifications include grades N-6, English 7-12, and Reading K-12. Her passion teaching struggling children to read led her to write a short chapter book, *The Last Wish**, about a boy who wishes his younger sister into a dragon's cave.

For the past twenty years, JoAnn has been writing teaching ideas and strategies for The Education Center's *Mailbox Magazines*. She also published a parent page for summer reading in Frank Schaffer's *Schooldays*. Recently, JoAnn wrote a bi-weekly column for the *Adirondack Journal* entitled *Giving Your Child an Edge*.

JoAnn lives in Adirondack, NY, with her husband, Lee, and their very loud Jenday Conure. They raised three beautiful daughters, Kathie, Sandi, & Debbie, and have been blessed with four delightful grandchildren: Brianna, Kristina, Andrew and Amber. They recently gained two step-grandchildren, Kristyn and Alex. The girls, grandchildren, and spouses (Dan & Rich) continue to reside on Long Island, much to JoAnn's dismay!

**The Last Wish has large print and less than seventy pages so frustrated readers are not overwhelmed and independent readers will delight. Young readers eagerly decode familiar words they have heard but not seen, thus building their reading vocabulary and strengthening reading skills as they share in the character's adventurous journey to rescue his sister. *The Last Wish* can be purchased on-line at amazon.com, barnesandnoble.com, and lulu.com or from JoAnn's website, joannflammer.com.